DIG AND DISCOVER
FOSSILS

by Anita Naht

CAPSTONE PRESS
a capstone imprint

Published by Capstone Press, an imprint of Capstone
1710 Roe Crest Drive, North Mankato, Minnesota 56003
capstonepub.com

Library of Congress Cataloging-in-Publication Data is available on the Library of
Congress website.
ISBN: 9781666342505 (hardcover)
ISBN: 9781666342529 (paperback)
ISBN: 9781666342536 (ebook PDF)

Summary: Sometimes the remains of plants and animals make impressions on rock
or are replaced by rock. This forms fossils. Uncover the variety of ways a fossil forms
and where you can search for these remains.

All internet sites appearing in back matter were available and accurate when this
book was sent to press.

DISCLAIMER:

This book provides information about various types of rocks and where and how to find them. Before
entering any area in search of rocks, make sure that the area is open to the public or that you have secured
permission from the property owner to go there. Also, take care not to damage any property, and do not
remove any rocks from the area unless you have permission to do so.

Rock hunting in riverbeds, quarries, mines, and some of the other areas identified in this book can be
inherently risky. You should not engage in any of these activities without parental supervision. Also, you
should always wear proper safety equipment and know how to use any tools that you bring with you. You
should not engage in any activity that is beyond your ability or skill or comfort level. Failure to follow
these guidelines may result in damage to property or serious injury or death to you or others, and may
also result in substantial civil or criminal liability.

The publisher and the author shall not be liable for any damages allegedly arising from the information
in this book, and they specifically disclaim any liability from the use or application of any of the contents
of this book.

CONTENTS

INTRODUCTION
BEFORE US 4

CHAPTER 1
MADE FOR THE FUTURE 6

CHAPTER 2
THROUGH THE AGES................................12

CHAPTER 3
THE HUNT FOR FOSSILS.........................16

CHAPTER 4
IS IT A FOSSIL? 24

CHAPTER 5
FOSSIL CARE...26

GLOSSARY.....................30
READ MORE..................31
INTERNET SITES............31
INDEX..........................32

Words in **bold** are in the glossary.

INTRODUCTION
BEFORE US

Millions of years ago, dinosaurs and other ancient creatures may have been roaming where you live today. They may have been flying through the air, stomping through forests, and fighting one another in fearsome battles.

We can't see dinosaurs today. They died out about 66 million years ago. But sometimes we find their preserved remains, or fossils. We can find other fossils too. We might find fossils of ancient plants or fish. They all could have lived where you live now. Fossils let us see how Earth has changed over time. **Paleontologists** study them. Some people collect them for fun. With proper planning and some luck, you might find a fossil too!

Some dinosaurs and other ancient creatures have left behind fossils that people can discover today.

CHAPTER 1
MADE FOR THE FUTURE

Dinosaur tracks. Tree wood turned into stone. Mammoth tusks. These are all fossils. Fossils are the preserved remains or traces of ancient life forms. They can be big or small. **Microbe** remains are so small they can't be seen without a microscope. Stromatolites are the oldest fossils. These ancient microbes are about 3.5 billion years old!

FACT

Coprolite is a trace fossil of animal poop. Scientists can learn a lot by studying it, such as what dinosaurs ate.

There are two kinds of fossils. A body fossil is from a life form's body. Teeth, bones, and leaves are body fossils. Trace fossils preserve a life form's activity. Footprints and nests are trace fossils.

Stromatolite Fossil
2.95 Billion Year Old
Cyanobacterial Layering

Stromatolite fossils form when a group of microbes traps tiny bits of rock. The rock forms layers, and the structure grows.

Many fossils, even at museums, are not complete. Scientists may use replicas of bones found with other fossils to create a full skeleton.

It's Hard!

Most dead plants and animals never become fossils. They rot, or other animals eat them. But hard body parts rot slowly. These include bones, teeth, and shells. Animals can't eat them easily. Hard body parts are the ones that normally become fossils.

You probably won't dig up a whole dinosaur skeleton. Vertebrate fossils are rare. A vertebrate is an animal with a backbone. These animals include dinosaurs, mammoths, and fish. Whole skeletons are even rarer. You might find bits of bone. But most likely, if you find an animal fossil, it will be from an invertebrate. These animals don't have backbones. Common fossils of this type are **ammonites** and **trilobites**. They were ancient sea creatures with shells.

Ammonite fossils are in a spiral shape.

Stuck!

Most fossils are of animals or plants that lived in or near water. Their bodies were quickly buried by **sediment**, such as mud. The mud and **minerals** turned to **sedimentary rock** around the fossil. Soft parts of the plant or animal rotted away. Then, water carrying minerals seeped into the remains. The minerals replaced the remains. This is called petrification.

In other cases, the remains left an outline in the rock. This is called a mold fossil. If minerals fill this outline, they form a cast fossil.

A cast fossil (left) has a raised surface. A mold fossil (right) is an imprint in the rock.

Amber can be found throughout the world but is most common near the Baltic Sea in Europe.

Rarely, fossils form in other ways. Animals and plants can get stuck in sticky substances. Ancient insects have been found in **amber**. Animals, plants, or their remains can freeze. Mammoth fossils have been found in glaciers. Animal and plant remains can dry out. A giant sloth fossil found in a cave was dried out like a raisin. These fossils can have preserved skin and hair.

FACT

Minerals can add color to fossils. You might find brassy pyrite, colorful agate, and more growing in your fossil!

CHAPTER 2
THROUGH THE AGES

Earth is about 4.5 billion years old. Its history can be divided into four major time periods. Each period had different life forms. The fossils from each time are different too.

We live in the Cenozoic Era. This is the Age of Mammals. It dates back 66 million years. Mammoth fossils are common from this time.

The Mesozoic Era was 66 million to 252 million years ago. It was the Age of Reptiles. Dinosaur and bird fossils are common.

The Paleozoic Era was 252 million to 541 million years ago. People often find sea life fossils from this time. Trilobites are common.

Before that was the Precambrian Era. This was the Age of Early Life. Stromatolite fossils are common.

Trilobite fossils are among the most common types of fossils.

FACT

Sir Richard Owen said the bones being dug up in England in the early 1800s came from "fearfully great" lizards. In 1842, he invented the name *Dinosauria* for them. We now call them dinosaurs.

Knowing the rock layer in which a fossil is found can help date the fossil.

How Old Is It?

New fossils and rock settle on top of old ones. You have to dig deeper to find older fossils. This timeline of fossils is called the fossil record. It helps scientists learn when and where animals and plants lived.

It also helps scientists find a fossil's age. They check the area for index fossils. These are common fossils with a known age. A fossil will be older than the ones above it but younger than those under it. This is why you shouldn't move a vertebrate fossil. It might be important for dating nearby fossils. Or the surrounding fossils might be needed to date it.

FACT FILE

Name: fossil
Life forms: animals, plants, early humans, and microbes
Types: body fossils such as teeth and bones; trace fossils such as burrows and tail drags
Ways of formation: petrification, molds, casts, trapped in amber or tar, frozen, or dried out
Location: all over the world, especially in places once covered by water and in sedimentary rock; mountains, riverbanks, beaches, deserts, and **badlands**
Size: microscopic, as with microbes, to more than 200 feet (60 meters), as with tree trunk fossils

CHAPTER 3
THE HUNT FOR FOSSILS

Finding a fossil is rare. Knowing where to look helps! Most fossils are in sedimentary rock. Quarries and mountains are good places to look. So are riverbanks, beaches, and deserts. Dry, rocky badlands are rich in fossils.

Some fossils are easier to find. Look for ammonites at the bases of cliffs near oceans and rivers. Check near streams and creeks in mountains for trilobites. Look for shark tooth fossils on the coastline. Petrified wood is common in deserts or dry creek beds.

Your timing helps too. Some fossils are easier to see after a storm. Check beaches at low tide. Look around creeks after floods dry up. The soil washes away to show what is underneath.

It can take time to find fossils on a beach.

A chisel can help remove rock, and a brush can gently sweep dirt off a fossil.

Get Ready

Are you ready to fossil hunt? You'll need some tools! You can dig with a small shovel. Bring a camera. Take photos of the fossil before you dig. Take photos of the area. This will show where the fossil came from.

Bring small plastic bags and a marker. Label a bag with the location and date. Wrap the fossil in toilet paper or newspaper to protect it. Put the wrapped fossil in the labeled bag. A large bag or pail can store your finds.

Dress for safety! Safety glasses will protect your eyes from debris. Wear gloves, long pants and sleeves, and closed-toe shoes. Wear a helmet near overhead cliffs. Carry a cell phone and compass. These will help keep you from getting lost. Take a first aid kit. Be careful, and always fossil hunt with an adult!

Fantastic Find!

In 1811, 12-year-old Mary Anning and her brother were looking for fossils in nearby cliffs to sell in England. They wanted to help earn money for their family. They had done this many times over the years, but this time they made an amazing discovery! They found and dug up the first skeleton of an Ichthyosaurus, a type of sea reptile. Over the years, Mary found more fossils no one had never seen before. Her fossils can still be seen in the Natural History Museum of London.

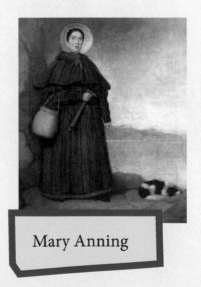

Mary Anning

The American West is rich in fossils. Some **rock hounds** travel to Wyoming, Utah, or Colorado. These states have fish fossils along the Green River.

There are other places with fossils too. Look for trilobites in Penn Dixie Fossil Park in New York. Fossil Park in Ohio has **brachiopod** and coral fossils. Do you want ancient shark teeth? Check Calvert Cliffs in Maryland. Visit Dinosaur Valley State Park in Texas. You'll see dinosaur tracks!

Some paleontologist digs are open to the public. You usually won't get to keep any fossils. But you can help scientists unearth rare fossils! You might also want to join a fossil club. Some sites let in only club members.

Follow the Rules

Know the rules before you go to a site. Most national sites don't allow fossil hunts. Look on private land only with the owner's permission. Some places limit when and where you can dig. Some limit how many fossils you can keep. Some ban selling them.

Theropod tracks are one type of dinosaur track found at Dinosaur Valley State Park.

Make sure you know the rules before you look for fossils to collect.

Most public places won't let you keep vertebrate fossils. Often, permits are given only to scientists. If you can get one, you may have to pay a fee. You may need to report your findings too.

If you find a fossil, let a paleontologist know. These scientists may work for the government, museums, or colleges. They keep track of fossils in your area.

Watch out for dangers. Don't go into bodies of water. Don't go into caves or mines or near cliff drop-offs.

National Fossil Day is celebrated every year. The holiday is on the Wednesday of the second full week in October.

Paleontologists can use your finds to learn more about ancient life in the area.

CHAPTER 4
IS IT A FOSSIL?

How do you know you've found a fossil? Some types are found only in rock. Some are only in sand. If you found it on the playground, could it be a fossil? Maybe, but probably not.

Check the color. Fossils are often a different color from the surrounding rock. Many are dark or colorful. Look at the texture. Bones have pores inside. Rocks don't. If the outside and inside are smooth, it's probably a rock.

Recent shark teeth are white, but fossilized shark teeth are darker in color.

Whole fossils often have certain shapes. Ammonites are spirals. Trilobites look like beetles. Ancient shark teeth are triangles.

Also check online guidebooks. Ask an adult to view the Association of American State Geologists website. This site links to state geology groups. Many share details about local fossils. If you're stuck, try asking your local museum for help.

Fantastic Find!

In England in 2021, 6-year-old Siddak Singh Jhamat was digging for worms in his garden. Imagine his excitement when he found something that looked like a tooth or a claw! He dug it out of the clay. With help from his dad's fossil club, he was able to identify his find. It was a horn coral fossil between 251 and 488 million years old!

CHAPTER 5
FOSSIL CARE

Is your fossil dirty? If the fossil is soft, gently clean it with a paint brush. A magnifying glass can help you see better as you work. Otherwise, clean it with a soft toothbrush and water outside. When in doubt, leave the fossil alone. You don't want it to break!

Some hard fossils can be polished in a rock tumbler. Petrified wood is hard. It can be tumbled for more than seven days. Don't tumble soft fossils. They'll break.

Store your fossils in a cool, dry place. Heat and damp air can damage them.

Polishing the faces of petrified wood can help bring out the colors and patterns.

Recording each fossil you find will help you keep track of your collection.

Keep a Record

A log will help you keep track of your fossils. Use a computer, index cards, or a notebook. Write the date and where the fossil was found. Include the map coordinates if possible. Add the fossil type, descriptions, and type of dirt or rock it was in.

Fossil hunting is about having fun. It's also about supporting science. Collect fossils with care. Avoid fossils you might damage. Don't touch vertebrate fossils. That way scientists can study them and learn about Earth's history. Maybe they'll even name a fossil after you!

FOSSIL CATALOG

DATE FOUND	FOSSIL TYPE	SIZE	COLOR	DESCRIPTION	SEDIMENT TYPE	LOCATION
8/28/2022	trilobite	1 inch long	dark gray	oval; cracked down the middle	shale rock	Penn Dixie Fossil Park, Blasdell, New York; GPS 42° 77' 80.47" N and 78° 83' 27.63" W

GLOSSARY

amber (AM-bur)—a yellow to brown, hardened, see-through fossilized tree resin

ammonite (AM-uh-nite)—a spiral-shaped fossil often found in marine rocks, dating from the Paleozoic to Mesozoic Era

badlands (BAD-lands)—areas with few plants and where the land has been worn away into many unusual rocky formations

brachiopod (BRAY-key-uh-pawd)—a sea invertebrate with two shells like a clam

microbe (MYE-krobe)—a small life form, such as a bacterium, that can be seen only under a microscope

mineral (MIN-ur-uhl)—a substance found in nature that is not made by a plant or animal

paleontologist (pay-lee-uhn-TAH-luh-jist)—a scientist who studies fossils and ancient life forms

rock hound (ROK HAUND)—someone who looks for and collects rocks as a hobby

sediment (SED-uh-muhnt)—a solid substance, such as sand, that is deposited by water, wind, or ice

sedimentary rock (sed-uh-MEN-tur-ee ROK)—rock that formed from layers of material like sand and dirt that were laid down and pressed together

trilobite (TRY-luh-bite)—a type of marine invertebrate from as early as the Paleozoic Era

READ MORE

Daniels, Patricia. *1,000 Facts About Dinosaurs, Fossils, and Prehistoric Life*. Washington, D.C.: National Geographic Kids, 2020.

Hudd, Emily. *How Long Does It Take to Make a Fossil?* North Mankato, MN: Capstone, 2020.

Petersen, Christine. *Unearth Fossils*. Minneapolis: Abdo, 2020.

INTERNET SITES

American Museum of Natural History: Paleontology: The Big Dig
amnh.org/explore/ology/paleontology

DK Find Out!: Fossils
dkfindout.com/us/dinosaurs-and-prehistoric-life/fossils/

Kentucky Geological Survey: Identifying Unknown Fossils
www.uky.edu/KGS/fossils/fossilid.php

Oxford University Museum of Natural History: Fossils
www.oum.ox.ac.uk/thezone/fossils/index.htm

INDEX

ammonites, 9, 16, 25

Anning, Mary, 19

cleaning, 26

clubs, 20, 25

dinosaurs, 4, 6, 9, 12, 13, 20

fossil formation, 10–11, 15

minerals, 10, 11

paleontologists, 4, 20, 22

record keeping, 28–29

rules, 20, 22

sedimentary rock, 10, 15, 16

Singh Jhamat, Siddak, 25

supplies, 18–19

trilobites, 9, 12, 16, 20, 25

ABOUT THE AUTHOR

Anita Nahta Amin is an author of children's books and short stories. She lives in Florida with her husband and twin children. She can often be found walking on the beach, watching the ships sail past. More information about her books can be found at www.AnitaAminBooks.com. She loves hearing from readers!

Editorial Credits
Editor: Marie Pearson; Designer: Joshua Olson; Production Specialists: Joshua Olson and Polly Fisher

Image Credits
Getty Images: Aptyp_koK, Cover, 1; Newscom: News Licensing /MEGA, 25; Science Source: 19, Charles R. Belinky, 10, David Woodfall Images, 14; Shutterstock: Adwo, 7, ArtEvent ET, 9, Artmim, 28, Bjoern Wylezich, 11, Eugen Thome, 13, Evgeny Haritonov, 23, Goldsithney, 17, Ivan Smuk, 24, Kues, (texture) design element throughout, Mariana Rusanovschi, 18, olpo, 27, Orla, middle 5, Steffen Foerster, bottom right 5, Tawnya92, 22, Vlad G, 8, W. Scott McGill, 21